CHRYSLER
MUSCLE CARS

Mike Mueller

Motorbooks International
Publishers & Wholesalers ®

You know what a Hemi is. Its got valves as big as stove lids. A plug jammed right in the middle of the combustion chamber. 426 cubes. And a thermal efficiency that is making a lot of people see red . . . taillights.

—*Dodge advertisement,* 1964

Acknowledgments

Many thanks go out to all the people who took the time to share their magnificent Mopars with the readers of this book. In order of appearance, they are:

George Shelley, Pompano Beach, Florida: Chrysler 300C convertible; Marvin and Joan Hughes, Ocala, Florida: 1957 Dodge D500 convertible; Gary Ogletree, Fayetteville, Georgia: 1958 Plymouth Fury; Ken Lanious, Forest Park, Illinois: 1959 Plymouth Sport Fury; Doug West, Preston, Idaho: 1959 DeSoto Adventurer; Paul Garlick, Lehigh Acres, Florida: 1961 Dodge Polara D500 convertible; Dan Heller, Tolono, Illinois: 1964 Chrysler 300K; Dennis Haak, Annville, Pennsylvania: 1960 Dodge Dart Phoenix D500; John Buxman, Eustis, Florida: 1962 Dodge Polara 413 Max Wedge; Bill and Barbara Jacobsen, Silver Dollar Classic Cars, Odessa: Florida, 1963 Dodge 330 426 Max Wedge; Steve Conti, St. Petersburg, Florida: 1969 Dodge Dart GTS; Garrett Bates, Pompano Beach, Florida: 1971 Dodge Demon; Bernie and Sheila Hage, Tampa, Florida: 1972 Plymouth Duster; Marvin and Joan Hughes, Ocala, Florida: 1966 Plymouth Belvedere II 426 Hemi; Roger and Janet Dunkelmann, Palm Beach Gardens, Florida: 1966 Dodge Charger 426 Hemi; Tony George, Clearwater, Florida: 1967 Plymouth GTX; Floyd Garrett, Fernandina Beach, Florida: 1968 Plymouth Road Runner 426 Hemi; Stuart Echolls, Lakeland, Florida: 1969 Dodge Super Bee 440 Six Pack; Bill and Barbara Jacobsen, Silver Dollar Classic Cars, Odessa, Florida: 1969 Dodge Daytona, 1969 Dodge Charger 500 426 Hemi, and 1970 Plymouth Superbird 426 Hemi; Steve Siegel, Lakeland, Florida: 1971 Dodge Charger R/T 426 Hemi; Jim Ludera, Bradenton, Florida: 1970 Plymouth Hemi 'Cuda; Robert Yappell, Princeton, Florida: 1970 Dodge T/A Challenger; Bill and Barbara Jacobsen, Silver Dollar Classic Cars, Odessa, Florida: 1970 Plymouth 'Cuda 440+6 and 1971 Dodge Challenger convertible.

ROAD RUNNER SUPERBIRD

© WARNER BROS.-SEVEN ARTS. INC.

Introduction

Performance, Mopar Style

Chrysler Corporation's modern performance roots can be traced back to the 1951 introduction of the innovative Firepower V-8, a powerful design that debuted in the DeSoto ranks in 1952, and then as a Dodge offering the following year. Featuring an efficient cylinder head using hemispherical combustion chambers, the Firepower "Hemi" represented an impressive entry in Detroit's burgeoning horsepower race even if the cars it powered weren't particularly intimidating.

Chrysler rectified that situation by rolling out its famed 300 "letter-series" luxury performance models in 1955. Taking its name from the 300hp 331ci Hemi beneath its hood, the 1955 C-300 was the "most powerful sedan in the world," according to *Mechanix Illustrated*'s Tom McCahill. In 1956, all Chrysler divisions made moves into the fast lane as DeSoto's Adventurer, Dodge's D500, and Plymouth's Fury appeared, each capable of running with Detroit's best.

By 1959, Chrysler had discontinued the Hemi in favor of lighter, less-complicated wedge-head V-8s. In 1960, the wedge-heads could be ordered with the exotic "ram-induction" setup—two four-barrel carburetors mounted outboard of each valve cover on long individual-runner manifolds. A variation on the ram-induction theme helped put

Opposite page
Plymouth's Superbird, basically a NASCAR racer unleashed on the street, was indicative of both how far Chrysler Corporation officials would go to stay on top of the performance heap and the degree of competitiveness reached by the muscle car crowd in the late sixties. With a 426 Hemi behind its aerodynamic snout and its distinctive "towel rack" rear spoiler, the Superbird was a certified 200mph screamer on the superspeedways. Hot on the heels of Dodge's winged Charger Daytona of 1969, the 1970 Superbird flew down the superspeedways for one year before racing's rulemakers shot it down.

Dodge and Plymouth atop the factory super-stock field in 1962. Featuring a compact cross-ram intake, the 413 "Max Wedge" was a direct response to Pontiac's 421 Super Duty and Chevrolet's 409. In 1963, an enlarged 426 Max Wedge appeared, followed by the Hemi's return in awesome 426ci race-only form in 1964.

Once the ball was rolling, there was no stopping Mopar performance; seemingly countless hot models began appearing in all model lines. Plymouth debuted their Barracuda in April 1964, beating Ford's Mustang to market by two weeks, and offering Mopar fans a pony car alternative to Dearborn's sales phenomenon. Enhancing the early Barracuda's performance image was 1965's Formula S version, a sporty handler equipped with a 235hp 273ci small-block V-8. At the same time, Dodge's compact Dart was developing as a potential performer, receiving the 383ci big-block in 1968, followed by an outrageous 440ci-equipped GTS model in 1969.

After NASCAR officials banned the 426ci race Hemi following the 1964 season, Chrysler engineers returned to the drawing board and penned the legendary 426ci street Hemi. Beginning in 1966, the Hemi was offered optionally for Dodge and Plymouth mid-sized models. That same year the stunning Charger first appeared in intermediate ranks. Joining the Charger in Dodge's 1967 performance stable was the hot-blooded, 440ci big-block-equipped Coronet R/T—a

muscle-bound package mirrored by Plymouth's 1967 GTX. Big news in 1968 came in the form of Plymouth's Road Runner and Dodge's Super Bee, each created as budget-minded supercars offering loads of performance with few frills.

In 1969, Dodge designers built two specially equipped models to homologate wind-cheating bodies for NASCAR competition. While the Charger 500 featured only a flush-mounted grille and rear window, the Charger Daytona represented a radical departure with its huge rear wing and lengthened snout. Plymouth applied similar tactics to the Road Runner in 1970, resulting in the Superbird.

Also new for 1969 was a 440 fed by three Holley two-barrel carburetors, known as the 440 Six Pack in Dodge trim, and the 440 Six Barrel when under Plymouth hoods. Special versions of the Road Runner and Super Bee models were built to showcase the tri-carb 440.

When the restyled E-body 'Cuda and Challenger appeared in 1970, either could be ordered with the triple-carb big-block or the dominating Hemi. The 440 option carried over into 1971, the last year before tightening emissions restrictions led to radical cutbacks. Although a few "unofficial" triple-carb 440s managed to slip into public hands in 1972, the 440 Six Pack, 440+6, and 426 Hemi were cancelled, signaling the end of Chrysler Corporation's glory days.

From 1966 to 1971, more than 11,000 426ci Hemi V-8s made their way into various Dodge and Plymouth intermediates and pony cars, with a few race-minded A-body Darts and Barracudas thrown in for good measure. Packing 425 real horses, the Hemi could transform almost any Mopar model into a 13sec boulevard bully. Ford fans can brag about their Cobra Jets, Chevy followers will forever worship the LS6 454, but for six years there was basically only one king of Main Street USA—the 426 Hemi.

Chapter 1

Going Fast in a Big Way

Letter Cars, Adventurers, and Golden Commandos

The logic behind the name was simple; the big car's 331ci Hemi V-8 produced 300hp—remarkable output for 1955—thus Chrysler's impressive luxury/performance sedan was named "300." Actually, the 1955 model was officially labelled "C-300" in honor of various Chrysler prototypes identified by monikers using the "C" prefix. Each succeeding model took on a letter of the alphabet, resulting in Chrysler's 300s being referred to as "letter cars."

Nomenclature aside, all 300s were incredible machines combining full-sized luxury with loads of power and healthy suspension componentry. Leather interiors were standard, and so was state-of-the-art performance. Even at 4,300lb, the C-300 could run 0–60mph in 9.6sec, only 0.5sec slower than the 1955 V-8 Corvette. Sales brochures called the C-300 "America's greatest performing motor car . . . with the speed of the wind, the maneuverability of a polo pony, the power to pass on the road safely." In 1956, the 300B became the first American car to surpass the magical one-horsepower-per-cubic-inch barrier, its optional 354ci Hemi V-8 pumping out an advertised 355hp.

Chrysler made an ill-advised attempt to offer fuel injection under the 300's hood in 1958, then dropped the big, heavy Hemi V-8

Opposite page
Although many questioned the 1961 Dodge Polara's looks, it's awfully tough to knock a glaring red convertible. Dodge's 1961 Polara was based on a 122in wheelbase—four inches longer than the lower-priced Dart—and was set apart from its lower echelon running mates by a revised tail with rocket-inspired taillights. Notice the small "500" badge to the right of the left taillight—the only outward clue of a 1961 D500's presence, though in 1961 chrome rockers and wheel opening trim were part of the package as well. D500s were also equipped with larger 8.20x15in tires.

Chrysler introduced a convertible 300 letter car in 1957, a model suited nicely to the totally new long, low, and wide body inspired by stylist Virgil Exner. While the previous two 300s in 1955 and 1956 borrowed their grilles from the prestigious Imperial, the restyled 1957 300 used a grille all its own. A functional scoop below each pair of headlights aided in brake cooling. Also new was improved ride and handling, courtesy of Chrysler's innovative torsion bar front suspension, and an enlarged 392ci Hemi V-8. According to *Motor Life*, the attractive 300C could run 0–60mph in 7.7sec.

in favor of the lighter wedge-head powerplant the following year. Ram induction became a standard feature in 1960, and the 413ci-powered 300G of 1961 was perhaps the strongest letter car offered. With 400hp and 495lb-ft of torque delivered at an incredibly low 2800rpm, the 300G was not for the timid. According to *Motor Trend*, "care needs to be exercised on accelerating turns from a dead stop to avoid trading ends, since the tremendous torque makes it very easy to get out of shape." After an eleven year reign as "America's most powerful production car," Chrysler's letter series ended with 1965's 300L.

Plymouth and DeSoto got in the luxury/performance act in 1956. Every bit as lavish as Chrysler's 300, DeSoto's Adventurer came on the scene with an exclusive dose of golden imagery, plush appointments, and awesome power courtesy of a 320hp 341ci Hemi V-8. A 1956 Adventurer ran 137mph on the sands of Daytona Beach and later turned a 144mph lap around the Chrysler proving ground track in Chelsea, Michigan. DeSoto continued to offer its high-powered, limited-edition performance sedan in hardtop and convertible form through 1959, after which the Adventurer nameplate became the commonplace label for the division's top models.

Plymouth tried a similar approach in 1956, introducing its own limited-edition performance model. Available in eggshell white only, the Fury carried its own share of golden imagery and was capable of kicking up some sand as well. Powered by a unique

Chrysler rolled out 484 300C convertibles (five for export) in 1957, a figure second only to the droptop 300K's total in 1964. Production of 300C hardtops totalled 1,737, with another thirty-one built for export. Full "300C" identification appeared on the lower rear quarters, while small "300" badges were found on the deck lid and in the grille.

240hp 303ci V-8, a Fury dashed down Daytona Beach at 124mph during speed tests in February 1956. Offered for three model runs in basically unchanged fashion, the Fury suffered the same fate as DeSoto's Adventurer, trading in its exclusive performance package for a role as Plymouth's flagship line in 1959.

Dodge's power brokers chose a different path. Instead of a high-profile, limited-edition muscle machine, they offered an optional performance package available for any model in the Dodge line from the Custom Royal

Chrysler's impressive 392ci Hemi V-8 was offered in two forms under the 300C's long hood: the 375hp standard with 9.25:1 compression and a 390hp version for $500 more. Included in the latter's power pack was a high-lift cam and increased compression (10:1). Behind either 392 Hemi was a three-speed manual or Torqueflite automatic transmission. The accordion-like unit at top center is the optional power brake booster.

Right
Following Chrysler's first letter car, the C-300, each succeeding 300 was identified in alphabetic progression, beginning with the 300B in 1956, the 300C in 1957, and so on. After the 300H came and went in 1962, Chrysler officials skipped over the letter "I" to avoid confusion with the Roman numeral "I." The last letter car, the 300L, appeared in 1965.

Lancer hardtop down to the Coronet sedan. Aimed at making Dodge a force in NASCAR competition, the 1956 D500 package included various heavy-duty components and a choice of two 315ci Hemi V-8s, one with 9.25:1 compression and a single Carter four-barrel rated at 260hp, another with two Carter four-barrels pumping out 295 horses. All that muscle translated into record-shattering D500 performances at Bonneville in 1956, as well as a third-place finish for Dodge in NASCAR Grand National competition that year. Although Dodge quickly fell from NASCAR's ranks, the D500 package carried on, still available on all models through 1961.

By the time the smaller, lighter Max Wedge Mopars hit the scene in 1962, full-sized performance from Dodge and Plymouth had all but faded away, leaving only Chrysler's 300 letter cars to carry on the legacy for three more years.

17

Because Dodge's hot D500 was an optional performance package, it could be found in any guise from mundane four-door sedan to sexy convertible. The D500 equipment was introduced in 1956 and offered in various forms until 1961. Estimates put total production for the six-year model run at a mere 3,000. Consequently, D500 convertibles, like this 1957 Coronet, are exceptionally rare. Unlike the initial 1956 rendition, which featured various heavy-duty chassis components such as big Chrysler brakes, the 1957 D500 used standard Dodge running gear.

Left
As with all D500-equipped Dodges, the only outward identification on this 1957 D500 Coronet convertible is the small "500" badge on the deck lid. *Motor Trend* tested a 1957 Coronet four-door sedan with the 285hp D500 package and recorded a 0–60mph run of 9.4sec and quarter-mile performance of 17.2sec at 79mph. *Sports Car Illustrated* hotfoots did *Motor Trend* one better at the wheel of a 1957 D500 two-door Coronet hardtop, running 0–60mph in 8.5sec with a 16.6 quarter-mile time. Terminal speed was 83mph. The attractive wire wheels on this rarely seen D500 convertible were dealer-installed options in 1957.

C hrysler Corporation began the muscle car era when it introduced its first V–8. The hemispherical head engine unleashed a performance war. . . .
—Randy Leffingwell,
American Muscle

Again, two levels of D500 performance were available in 1957. This 285hp 325ci D500 V-8 featured solid lifters, 10:1 compression, and a single Carter four-barrel carburetor. Top of the heap was the Super D500, a 310hp version of the 325ci Hemi fed by twin Carter four-barrels. Price for the basic D500 powertrain option was $113.65. *Sports Car Illustrated* called the 285hp D500 V-8 "a well-balanced engine—not so big that it won't rev, and not so small that it lacks torque. As a result it delivers plenty of usable horsepower all the way up the line."

Offered in nearly identical, exclusive fashion from 1956 to 1958, Plymouth's Fury featured one shade only—Buckskin Beige (1956 models were eggshell white), a color not available on any other model. A complete array of golden imagery inside and out complemented this soft shade. At $3,032, this 1958 Fury was the only Plymouth that year priced above $3,000. Production in 1958 was 5,303, following totals of 7,438 in 1957 and 4,485 in 1956.

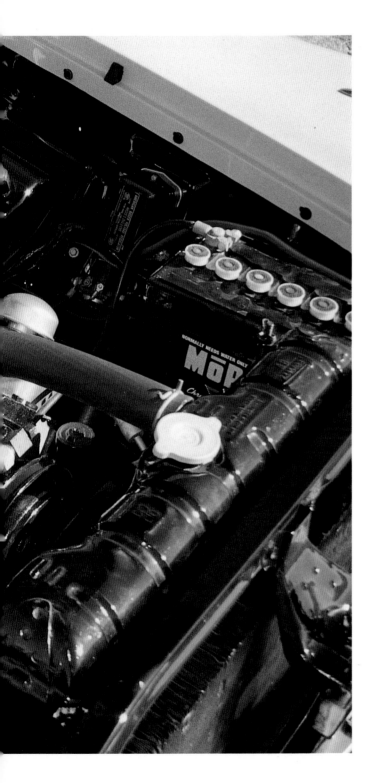

DeSoto offered its last limited-edition Adventurer luxury/performance cruiser in 1959. Standard features included power steering, power brakes, a padded dash, and a distinctive brushed aluminum sidesweep done in gold. In typical fashion, gold dress-up was also found in the grille and on the wheel covers. Inside, swivel bucket seats were introduced in 1959 as another standard Adventurer feature. Beneath the hood was a 350hp 383ci V-8 topped with two Carter four-barrel carburetors. Only 590 Adventurer hardtops were built in 1959, accompanied by a mere ninety-seven convertibles.

Left
Standard power for the 1957 and 1958 Fury was the "Dual Fury V-800" (shown here), a high-performance 318ci powerplant not available under other Plymouth hoods. Twin Carter four-barrels, 9.25:1 compression, a high-lift cam, a dual-point distributor, and dual exhausts all added up to 295hp. In 1958, the Dual Fury V-800 was joined by the optional Golden Commando 350ci V-8 rated at 305hp. The 1958 Golden Commando V-8 option was priced at $324 and offered on all Plymouth models.

Previous pages
Plymouth diluted the Fury image considerably in 1959, transferring the once-proud nameplate to its topline models, which meant a four-door Fury would hit the streets for the first time. Preserving some of the previous limited-edition image was the new Sport Fury, offered in two-door hardtop and convertible form. Sport Fury buyers were also presented with a wide array of color choices. Power came from a "Fury V-800" powerplant with "Super Pak"—a 260hp 318ci V-8 featuring a high-lift cam, 9:1 compression, free-flowing dual exhausts, and a Carter AFB four-barrel carburetor. Another reminder of the early Fury was the optional Golden Commando 395 V-8, an engine named for the 395lb-ft of torque it delivered.

Plymouth's Golden Commando V-8 was a $74 option displacing 361ci and making 305hp with the aid of 10:1 compression, a high-lift cam, special low-restriction dual exhausts, and a Carter four-barrel. Gold dress-up on the air cleaner and valve covers helped preserve the Fury tradition.

Right
Dodge's D500 option was available in a variety of forms in 1960 and 1961 and could be fitted to either the topline Polaras or the shorter, less prestigious Darts. In 1961, the "Dart D500" powerplant was a 305hp 361ci V-8, while the Polara version was based on the larger 383ci engine, both with single four-barrel carburetors. The wire wheels are a dealer-installed option.

In 1960, all D500 Dodges, Polara or Dart, featured the intriguing ram-induction setup with its long, spider-like manifolds. Offered for the last time in 1961, the D500 option was still available in ram induction form, but the basic package relied on a single Carter four-barrel carburetor on a conventional intake, as shown here. The "Polara D500" V-8 was a 383ci powerplant rated at 325hp with 10:1 compression. Polara D500s mated to the Torqueflite automatic came standard with 3.23:1 rear gears. Reportedly, a 1961 Polara D500 could hit 60mph from rest in 8.9sec.

No one did gadgetry better than the Chrysler Corporation. This fully loaded 1961 Polara convertible features a speedometer that allowed natural light to shine through for illumination, a rectangular steering wheel (for increased leg room), and the optional "Hi-Way Hi-Fi," a record player mounted beneath the dash above the transmission tunnel.

Left
The 1964 300K is considered by many to be the last great Chrysler 300 as its successor, the 1965 300L, was toned down considerably in the performance department. The 300K was the last letter car offered with the exotic ram-induction option, which looked every bit as impressive as it performed. Production of 300K hardtops reached 3,022, the highest total in the eleven-year letter-car history. Convertible production in 1964 was 625.

Standard power for the 1964 300K came from a 360hp 413ci big-block V-8 fed by a single four-barrel. Available at extra cost was a 390hp 413 topped by twin Carter AFB four-barrels on spider-like ram-induction aluminum intake manifolds. Introduced as a standard 300 feature in 1960, ram induction made its final appearance under the 300K's hood. Compression for the 390hp ram-induction 413, at 9.6:1, was actually lower than the 360hp, single-four-barrel version, which squeezed fuel and air at a 10:1 ratio.

Chapter 2

The A Team

Darts, Demons, & Dusters

A Dodge named Dart first appeared as a radically aerodynamic showcar in 1956. Four years later, the Dart returned as a new downsized regular production model rolling on a 118in wheelbase, four inches shorter than Dodge's Polara flagship. Also new for 1960 was unitized body construction and an impressive powertrain option called ram-induction. A "poorman's supercharger" of sorts, ram-induction helped make Dodges and Plymouths formidable forces at the dragstrip, establishing a legacy that grew in prominence with each passing year.

Another downsizing maneuver and further development of the ram-induction design in 1962 raised the racing stakes even higher. A smaller, lighter Dart based on a 116in wheelbase established the platform parameters, while the outrageous 413ci Max Wedge supplied the power. Crowned with a considerably more compact cross-ram intake, the Max Wedge V-8 transformed Dodges and

Plymouths into intimidating 13sec super-stocks right off the truck. A 1962 Plymouth Max Wedge eventually became the first "production car" to break the 12sec quarter mile barrier. A second-edition 1963 Max Wedge displacing 426ci left the competition even further behind.

That same year, Dodge transferred the Dart banner to a new compact model leading up to the development of Chrysler's A-body family. Initially offered only with six-cylinder

Opposite page
Perhaps the most nimble of Dodge's high-profile 1969 "Scat Pack," which included the R/T versions of the Charger and Coronet, the Dart GTS could be quickly identified by its standard twin hood bulges, various emblems, and twin exhaust trumpets. Popular "bumblebee" stripes for the tail were available at extra cost. Changes for 1969 included transferring the formerly standard GTS Dart's bucket seats to the options list.

Dodge's new 1960 Dart was smaller and less expensive than the topline Polara and possessed some serious performance potential when equipped with the D500 option. First made available in 1956, Dodge's D500 performance package was offered for Polaras and the three Dart models, Seneca, Pioneer, and Phoenix. Most prominent among D500 equipment in 1960 was the new ram-induction setup featuring twin four-barrels on long, individual-runner aluminum intake manifolds. In Polara ranks, the D500 option was available for the 383ci V-8, while Darts used a smaller 361ci version, though apparently it was possible to order the Polara's big 383ci D500 V-8 in the smaller Dart. *Sports Car Illustrated* wrote that a ram-inducted 1960 Dart "can make other road users a trifle sheepish at stop light showdowns."

power, the Dart GT first flexed a little muscle in 1964 when the 273ci small-block V-8 was made an option. Things really got hot four years later when the 275hp 340ci V-8 was introduced. The 340 was standard equipment for the 1968 Dart GTS and transformed Dodge's A-body into a serious quarter-mile threat, a fact *Car Life* verified with a 14.68sec ET topping out at 96.2 mph. And if that wasn't enough, the optional 383ci big-block promised even more. At the top of 1968's A-body heap was the awesome Hurst built, Hemi-powered Dart, an all-out racing counterpart to Plymouth's Hemi Barracudas.

In 1969, Dodge offered a 440-powered Dart GTS, a boulevard brute inspired by transplants performed by Chicago's legendary Mopar performance mogul Norm Krause, alias "Mr. Norm," of Grand-Spaulding Dodge. Roughly 600 440 GTS Darts were built in 1969, again with the help of the Hurst crew.

Contrasting with the big-block A-bodies was the new Dart Swinger 340, the smallest and most affordable member of Dodge's 1969 Scat Pack. Ads described the 275hp Swinger 340 as "6000 rpm for less than $3,000." *Car Life's* staff was so impressed with the Swinger 340's performance (14.8sec at 96mph in the quarter-mile) that they named it their "Best Compact" for 1969.

Inspired by Plymouth's success with the A-body Duster 340, a performance car for the budget-minded, Dodge designers traded the Swinger 340 for the Demon 340 in 1971. Plymouth's Duster 340 was introduced in 1970 and based on a Valiant platform with a

"fastback" of sorts grafted on. When equipped with the yeoman 340 small-block, both the Duster and Demon were capable of low-14sec blasts down the quarter-mile, putting them among Detroit's best bangs for the buck as the seventies dawned.

With performance de-escalation coming after 1971, Mopar's A-team was eventually disbanded; Dodge's Demon was gone by 1973, which was the last year for the 340. Armed with the optional 360ci small-block, Plymouth's Duster carried on in 1974, along with a Dart Sport counterpart from Dodge, but it just wasn't the same.

Since the D500's long ram-induction manifolds created a supercharging effect, this hot 361ci V-8 didn't require a major dose of high compression to up the power ante. At 10:1, the 1960 361ci Dart D500 V-8's compression level was typical for the day. Output was 310hp and 435lb-ft of torque, which translated into 0–60mph in the 8sec range. Mid-range power, however, was the D500's forte. As *Motor Trend*'s Walt Woron wrote, "the response when both carburetors cut in is instantaneous. It comes on with a roar, pushing you back in your seat, and the car leaps ahead like a ram rushing to butt a challenger."

Left
The small, vertical "500" badge on the deck lid of this 1960 Dart Phoenix was the only giveaway to this Dodge's status as a dominating D500 street warrior. Offered for the last time in 1961, the D500 option was toned down with a standard four-barrel offering in addition to the now optional ram-induction version (in 1960, all D500s were ram-induction cars). Reportedly only about 3,000 D500s were built between 1956 and 1961.

Two versions of the 413 Max Wedge were offered to Plymouth and Dodge buyers in 1962, the difference in output determined by the compression ratio chosen. The 410hp version featured 11:1 compression, while the 420hp 413 squeezed the mixture to the tune of 13.5:1. "Max" referred to the Maximum Performance label used in factory brochures, "Wedge" described the 413's wedge-shaped combustion chambers (as opposed to Dodge's earlier Hemispherical design). In Dodge ranks, the 413 Max Wedge was offered in all models from the bare-bones Dart 330 to the trimmed-out Polara 500. Since most racers preferred the lighter, cheaper Darts, Max Wedge Polaras like this one are exceptionally rare. Total production for all 1962 Max Wedges, Dodge and Plymouth, was about 300.

Previous pages
Priced at $374.40, the 410hp 413 was as affordable as it was powerful, leading *Motor Trend*'s Roger Huntington to claim it offered "more performance per dollar than any other factory-assembled car in America." Huntington also liked the Max Wedge's free-flowing cast-iron headers, calling them "a work of art—far and away the most efficient ever put on an American car." Behind those headers was a dual exhaust system that featured cutouts that could be unbolted for unsilenced, wide-open running. During Huntington's road test, a 1962 Max Wedge Dodge managed 0–60mph in 5.8sec and produced a 14.4sec, 100mph quarter-mile ET. With the exhaust cutouts unbolted and optional 9in tires in back, the car eventually turned a sizzling 13.44sec, 109.76mph ET.

Manufactured under precise conditions at Chrysler's Marine and Industrial Division, the 413 Max Wedge V-8 was a no-nonsense racing powerplant not intended for everyday operation. Heavy-duty dual valve springs in the heads meant valve seals couldn't be installed, making the Max Wedge a serious oil burner, but lubricant consumption was of no concern to a drag racer. Everything else about the Max Wedge was bullet-proof from top to bottom. A reinforced block and heads, a forged steel crank, Magnafluxed forged steel connecting rods, lightweight aluminum pistons, beefed-up valvetrain, and a deep-sump oil pan added up to one formidable powerplant. Topping it off were two Carter AFB carbs mounted diagonally on a cross-ram intake featuring 15in individual runners.

With the Dart nameplate moved down to Dodge's compact ranks, most 1963 Max Wedges appeared as stripped-down, inexpensive 330 models, with a few upscale Polaras again thrown in for good measure. New for 1963 was an optional, weight-saving aluminum front end with a distinctive scooped hood. The light front end helped trim the car's weight to 3200 pounds, which in turn made the 1963 426 Max Wedge Dodge an easy 12sec performer. As 1963 advertisements claimed, "when a Dodge loses these days, it's to another Dodge."

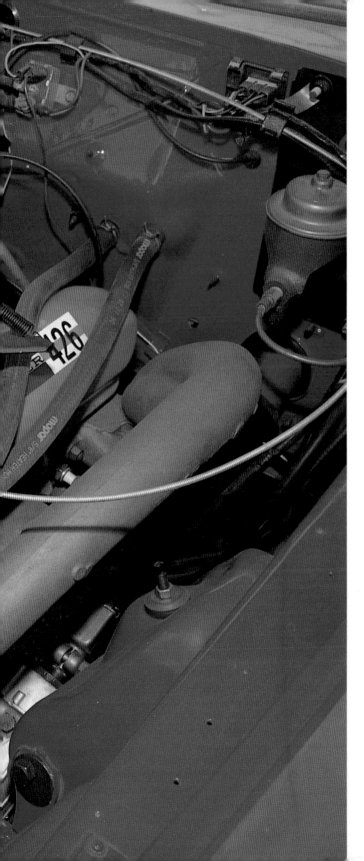

No extra baggage here; this 1963 Dodge 330 was meant for racing, not impressing the neighbors. Notice the dash-mounted push button transmission controls directly to the left of the steering wheel. Chrysler Corporation's excellent three-speed Torqueflite was Detroit's first automatic transmission capable of standing up to serious torque loads. From the beginning, automatic-backed Max Wedge Mopars were kings of drag racing's Stock/Automatic classes.

Left
Under Dodge hoods, the 413 or 426 Max Wedge was known as a "Ramcharger" V-8; Plymouth used the "Super Stock" moniker. As in 1962, the 426 Ramcharger V-8 for 1963 was offered in two forms, one with 11:1 compression and 415hp, the other with a head-cracking 13.5:1 squeeze and 425 horses. The two foam rubber "doughnuts" atop the carburetors sealed to the aluminum hood's underside allowing the functional scoop to supply cooler, denser air directly into the twin Carter AFBs.

43

Left
Dodge had offered a GT package for its compact Dart since the car's introduction in 1963, but early Dart GTs offered more sporty flair than actual performance. Then along came the 1968 Dart GTS, or GTSport. With a 275hp 340 as standard equipment, the Dart GTS was more than capable of holding its own. And for only $25 more, the 340 could've been traded for a 383ci big-block. This 1969 GTS 340 hardtop is one of 3,919 built.

Simulated vents in the twin hood bulges announced the GTS Dart's underhood contents, in this case the standard 275hp 340ci small-block, a popular powerplant that appeared throughout the Mopar muscle car ranks from 1968 to 1973. A collection of heavy-duty suspension equipment complemented the affordable, easy-to-handle 340 as part of the GTS performance package.

Left
Dodge introduced the Demon a year after Plymouth's Duster debuted in 1970. In the best GTS tradition, the Demon 340 was everything its A-body forerunners were and more. Along with the 275hp small-block, the Demon 340 came standard with a heavy-duty three-speed manual, Rallye suspension consisting of beefed-up torsion bars and a stiffer sway bar up front, heavier leaves in back, and upgraded shocks all around. A long list of options could both dress up the Demon 340 and punch up the power. But even in base form a Demon could turn the quarter in about 14.5sec. The tires, widened rear rims, and locking gas cap on this Panther Pink 1971 Demon 340 are owner-installed modifications.

From its 1968 inception, Mopar's 340ci small-block was a performance-minded powerplant that offered punch without the weight disadvantage typical to the 383ci big-block. Advertised output was 275hp at 5000rpm and 340lb-ft of torque at 3200rpm. Compression was 10.3:1. Production of Demon 340s in 1971 reached 10,098.

W e decided to make it a sleeper that would blow the doors off hulking, pretentious behemouths twice its size.

—1970 Plymouth brochure

Probably most commonly seen in E-body Barracudas and Challengers in 1971, this dictation recorder with its remote microphone wasn't exactly the type of performance equipment you'd expect to find in a 340-powered Dodge Demon.

Right
Plymouth rejoined Mopar's A-body performance ranks in 1970 with the Duster 340, a hot model that quickly qualified as a candidate for the Rapid Transit System, Plymouth's version of Dodge's Scat Pack. As advertisements explained, the Rapid Transit System wouldn't accept "any car that can't cut a 14-second quarter." According to *Car and Driver*, a 1970 Duster 340 put up a 14.39sec, 97.2mph ET—case closed. Production of 1972 Duster 340s, like this fully loaded Plum Crazy model, was 15,681.

This 8000rpm hood tach was among the many options available to Duster 340 buyers. Although both Demons and Dusters were affordable performance machines in base form, they got expensive in a hurry once buyers started checking-off boxes on the order sheet. A twin-scooped hood, rear spoiler, and Rallye wheels were among the most popular A-body add-ons.

Left
With real performance on the wane by 1971, splashy graphics and assorted imagery pieces became more popular. This blacked-out hood with "340 Wedge" identification was one of many available A-body dress-up items. Even in net-rated 240hp form, the Duster 340's small-block was still a hot little number in 1972.

Chapter 3

'Cudas & Challengers

Chrysler Corporation's Pony Cars

Even though Plymouth actually beat Ford to market by two weeks with its Barracuda, it was Dearborn's wildly popular Mustang that helped inspire the "pony car" label for the new long-hood/short-deck automotive breed. Introduced in April 1964, Plymouth's first pony car was basically a Valiant with a large glass "fastback" tacked on, an image that nonetheless came off remarkably fresh. Performance, however, was timid, at least until the Formula S version appeared in 1965. The S sported a 235hp 273ci Commando V-8, heavy-duty suspension, and four Goodyear Blue Streaks on wide 14in wheels.

A totally restyled Barracuda based on a larger A-body platform emerged in 1967, making room for Dodge's 383ci big-block V-8, a 280hp option for the Formula S and standard Barracudas. The following year, the Formula S model's base 273ci V-8 was exchanged for the hot little 275hp 340ci small-block, a derivative of the 273. According to *Car Life*, a 1968 340 Barracuda could trip the lights at the far end of the quarter-mile in 14.97sec.

Hottest of the A-body Barracudas were the 1968 Super Stock models. Armed with 425 Hemi horses, Super Stocks were capable of 10sec blasts down the quarter right out of the box. At least fifty of these race-ready Hemi Barracudas were built by Hurst in

Opposite page
Although it retained the previous A-body Barracuda's 108in wheelbase, just about everything else on Plymouth's new E-body platform represented a radical departure from past Mopar pony car practices. To emphasize the E-body's sporty image, Chrysler introduced a wild array of radiant paint schemes with equally wild names, including such shades as Go-Mango, Sublime, In Violet, and Plum Crazy. This Hemi-powered 1970 'Cuda hardtop is one of 284 built with a four-speed—another 368 were equipped with Torqueflites.

Under the direction of the Chrysler Advanced Styling Studio's Cliff Voss, designers began work in 1967 on the totally new, third-generation Barracuda. The bulk of the credit for Plymouth's exciting 1970 pony car goes to stylist John Herlitz. Three models were offered, the Barracuda and the upscale Gran Coupe, both powered by six-cylinders in base-form, and the 'Cuda, which featured a 335hp 383ci big-block as standard equipment. Optional 'Cuda performance powerplants included the 275hp 340ci small-block, the 375hp 440ci four-barrel, the 390hp 440+6 (with three Holley two-barrels) and the 425hp 426ci Hemi.

Detroit. Better suited for the street, yet still not meant for the meek, the 1969 'Cuda 440 featured 375hp and 480lb-ft of torque. A bit tough to live with as an everyday driver as power steering and power front discs couldn't be included due to space restrictions, the 440 'Cuda was nonetheless a certified 13sec street killer.

Mopar's pony car line-up received a totally new E-body shell in 1970 as Plymouth's Barracuda was joined by Dodge's Challenger, a small sporty package that resembled its corporate cousin but was two inches longer. Honoring the long-hood/short-deck theme to even greater extremes than their predecessors, the revitalized Barracuda and newborn Challenger turned heads with ease.

The huge Shaker hood scoop, standard on Hemi 'Cudas, was functional, but also assisted greatly in the image department. With the Shaker removed, the 426 Hemi's twin Carter AFB (aluminum four-barrel) carburetors are revealed. Hemi 'Cuda performance was simply awesome—according to *Car Craft*, the quarter-mile flew by in 13.10sec. Trap speed was 107.1mph.

High-back buckets, the distinctive "Tuff" steering wheel, and the trademark Pistol Grip four-speed shifter added a sporty touch to the 1970 Hemi

'Cuda's interior. Also visible are a 150mph speedometer and 8000rpm tach.

As for beauty beneath the skin, both Mopar E-bodies were available with an incredible variety of performance options, beginning with the potent 340 small-block, escalating up to the 383 big-block, going overboard with a 440+6 or 440 Six Pack, and peaking with the awesome 426 Hemi. At one end of the scale, 340 'Cudas and Challengers were quick, nimble road cars; at the other end, the nose-heavy 440 and Hemi cars were boulevard brutes with one thing in mind: travelling a straight line from point A to point

B as rapidly as possible. During the muscle car's heyday from 1970 to 1971, they didn't come much quicker than a Hemi-powered E-body Mopar.

The Hemi fell by the wayside after 1971, but 'Cudas and Challengers carried on in relatively sporty fashion, with the still-warm 340 small-block representing the hottest under-hood option. Like the brutish big-block V-8s, convertible E-bodies were discontinued after 1971, and the Barracuda/Challenger line itself appeared for the last time in 1974.

Created to homologate a road racing relative for SCCA Trans Am competition, Dodge's T/A Challenger hit the streets in March 1970. T/A Challengers were powered by a 340 Six Pack small-block V-8 unique to the application and equipped with a host of standard performance equipment including heavy-duty suspension, a Hurst-shifted four-speed, and racing-type cutout exhausts. Ads promised a second T/A Challenger rendition in 1971, but the idea was cancelled in 1970. Only 2,399 T/As were built. Another 2,724 nearly identical AAR (a reference to Dan Gurney's "All American Racing" team which built and raced the Trans Am version) 'Cuda models were produced for 1970.

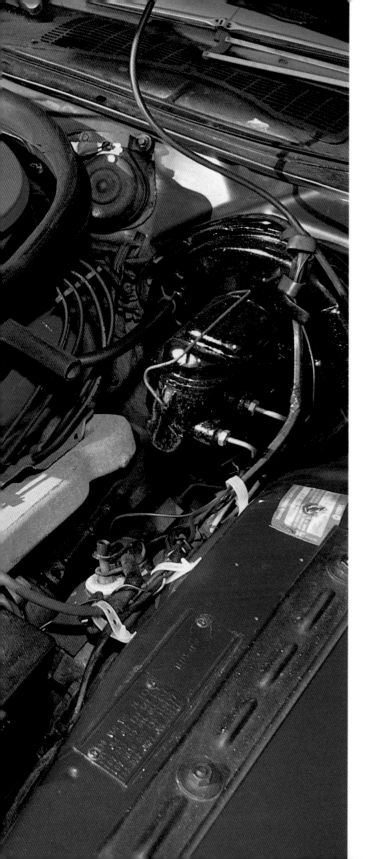

Dodge's T/A Challenger and Plymouth's AAR 'Cuda were probably the first Detroit performance machines with mismatched rubber—G60 Goodyear tires in back, E60s in front (this car has non-stock aftermarket treads). Although most T/A Challengers wear the optional Rallye wheels, the standard rims were these 15x7JJ steel units with center caps and trim rings. Also standard were cutout exhausts, which helped in the image department but did little for performance since the exhaust plumbing required to make the system work, was overly restrictive. Many owners dumped this arrangement in favor of a conventional rear-exiting system.

Left
Built from the oil pan up as a serious performance power-source, the 340 Six Pack featured a recast block with a reinforced lower end, reworked cylinder heads with ample room for porting, a beefed-up valvetrain, and 10.5:1 compression. Three Holley two-barrels on an aluminum Edelbrock intake fed the beast. Output was conservatively listed at 290hp, 15hp more than the equally underrated standard 340 four-barrel V-8. Actual Trans Am racing Challengers were powered by a destroked 305ci version of the 340 and produced an amazing 440hp.

A large rubber gasket around the 340 Six Pack V-8's air cleaner sealed the unit to the underside of this fiberglass hood, allowing cooler denser air to flow through its racing-style snorkel scoop directly to the three Holleys. Engineers discovered that elevating the scoop's snout about one inch above the hood helped circumvent the induction-inhibiting boundary layer of slow-moving air that normally develops at speed, a trick that was reportedly worth another 10 or 15hp at 80mph.

Right
Helping set the hotter 1970 'Cuda models apart from their sedate Barracuda and Gran Coupe brethren were standard fog lights below the bumper and a sport hood with twin scoops. The eye-catching Shaker hood, a standard feature on Hemi 'Cudas, was optional with all other V-8s. 'Cudas also included various heavy-duty suspension pieces. In back, beefy leaf springs featured five full leaves with two half leaves on the left, and six full leaves on the right. Stiffer shocks all around and thicker 0.92in torsion bars up front working in concert with an enlarged 0.94in stabilizer bar helped keep all that torque under control. The popular Rallye wheels were optional. This 1970 440+6 'Cuda hardtop, one of 1,755 built, features the Shaker hood as well as the "hockey stick" engine identification stripes on the rear quarter

Hiding beneath this 1970 'Cuda's Shaker scoop are three Holley two-barrels atop the impressive 390hp 440 big-block. Under Plymouth pony car hoods, this setup was known as the 440+6; identical Dodge versions wore the 440 Six Pack label. Internal features of the 440+6 included a forged-steel crank, heavy-duty connecting rods, and reinforced, cast-aluminum 10.5:1 pistons.

The unforgettable Shaker scoop did just that—lurching and shaking considerably when a 440+6 'Cuda's pedal went to the metal. Offered in Argent Silver, matte black or body color, Shakers were standard atop 426 Hemis and optional on all other 1970–71 'Cuda and Challenger V-8s.

Following pages
With its 110-inch wheelbase stretched two inches longer than its E-body counterpart from Plymouth, Dodge's Challenger differed just enough to not be accused of being a rubber-stamp mirror image. Sheet metal differences between the Challenger and 'Cuda were considerable. The Challenger's most unique exterior features are its beltline crease and quad headlights. Convertible E-bodies were built for 1970 and 1971 only; this Plum Crazy 1971 Challenger droptop is one of 2,165 built.

I t snarls, it quivers,
it leaps vast prairies at a
single bound.
—1970 Challenger brochure

Standard power source for the Challenger R/T
("Road and Track"), the 383 Magnum V-8 was
optional for all other Challengers. Mandated
decompression dropped the 383 Magnum's
output from 335hp in 1970 to 300hp in 1971,
but the aging big-block was still one tough
customer under an E-body's hood. Reportedly,
only 126 1971 Challenger convertibles were
built with the 383 Magnum backed by the
Torqueflite automatic.

When fully equipped with all the optional goodies like buckets, console with floor shift, and a sport steering wheel, Challengers were as sporty inside as they were out. The orange knob below the dash at the head of the console controlled the Shaker hood scoop's cool air induction system.

Chapter 4

Big, Bad B-Bodies

Mopar's Mid-Sized Muscle

Chrysler Corporation's all-out 1964 426ci race Hemi enjoyed only one race season before NASCAR moguls killed it with a change to the minimum production homologation requirements. Chrysler's initial response was to pull out of NASCAR racing for the 1965 season, but the Mopar crew returned in 1966 following development of a new, "detuned" 426 Hemi. The new engine was built with everyday street operation in mind, if only to appease sanctioning bodies who liked to see so-called stock cars race in stock classes.

Although the 426ci street Hemi was indeed detuned in comparison to its racing forefather, it was by no means emasculated. *Motor Trend* noted that "you can buy Plymouth's intermediate-sized Belvedere, right off the showroom floor, with a '426 Hemi' and have a darn good chance of winning [your] class in A/ or AA/Stock [drag racing] right off the bat with only minor modifica-

tions." With 425hp on tap, the 426 Hemi immediately transformed all Mopar B-bodies into high-13sec screamers.

Most stylish among the early high-powered B-bodies was Dodge's Charger, which

Opposite page
Introduced mid-year in 1969, Dodge's Six Pack Super Bee was the epitome of no-frills performance. Wheel covers weren't even included in the package, nor were hood hinges— the fiberglass hood with its huge functional scoop simply lifted off once pins were released at all four corners. Beneath that hood was a 390hp 440 big-block topped by three Holley two-barrels. In exchange for an incredibly low $3,138 asking price, Six Pack Super Bee customers received a streetwise strip challenger capable of turning 13.8sec quarters. Dodge built 817 Six Pack Super Bee hardtops like this one in 1969 and another 615 coupe versions. Plymouth also offered a similar 440 Six Barrel Road Runner for 1969. The non-functional rear quarter scoops shown here were optional pieces.

The famed 426 street Hemi debuted in 1966 to rave reviews and was available in Dodge Chargers and Coronets and Plymouth Belvederes and upscale Satellites. Test drive results varied, with *Car and Driver's* 13.80sec quarter-mile dash in a 1966 Hemi Satellite ranking among the quickest. This gold 1966 Plymouth Belvedere II convertible is one of only six equipped with the 425hp 426 Hemi and Torqueflite automatic transmission that year. Four other 1966 Hemi Satellite convertibles were built with four-speeds.

was basically a mundane Coronet shell radically transformed through the addition of hideaway headlights and a sloping fastback roofline. Introduced along with the street Hemi in 1966, the Charger's interior featured four bucket seats and a console. Not nearly as radical but equally sporty, Plymouth's GTX appeared in 1967 showcasing a new pumped-up 375hp version of the 440ci big-block V-8 introduced the previous year, a power source that offered almost as much performance potential as the Hemi for a fraction of the cost.

In 1968, Plymouth and Dodge kicked off the "budget supercar" race, introducing the Road Runner and Super Bee, respectively. The base-model versions of these hot B-bodies were bare-bones bombers with frills spared in favor of pure performance. Standard equipment included a specially prepared 335hp 383ci big-block backed by a four-speed. Price was just short of $3,000, and quarter mile performance measured just this side of 100mph. Carrying the budget supercar idea one step further, Dodge and Plymouth introduced the Six Pack Super Bee and Six Barrel Road Runner for 1969, each a stripped-down, strip-ready racer with 390 horses beneath a lift-off fiberglass hood.

B-body aggression escalated to an even higher level in 1969 with the coming of Dodge's NASCAR-inspired aero fliers, the Charger 500 and Charger Daytona. Built to homologate wind-cheating variants for competition on NASCAR's superspeedways, the Charger 500 featured a blunt nose with a

flush-mounted grille and a similar treatment in back where the standard Charger's drag-intensive tunneled backlight was traded for flush-mounted glass. Although the tricks improved the B-body's high-speed characteristics, the Charger 500 still wasn't the answer to Ford's challenge on the NASCAR circuit, a

The radical 426 race Hemi had featured individual-tube headers and twin carbs mounted diagonally on a cross-ram intake, but 1966's slightly civilized street Hemi was equipped with a more conventional inline, dual four-barrel intake and cast-iron exhaust manifolds. Output was 425hp at 5500rpm and 480lb-ft of torque.

"Leader of the Dodge Rebellion" was how advertisements labeled the exciting 1966 Dodge Charger. Like Plymouth's little Barracuda, which was basically a Valiant with a huge rear window tacked on, Dodge's Charger was essentially a ho-hum Coronet under that sloping fastback and behind those hideaway headlights, a resemblance made more obvious when the lights were exposed. Nonetheless, the look came off remarkably well. Inside, the Charger was far from ho-hum with four buckets and a long console as standard sporty features. When armed with the optional 426 Hemi, all that sporty imagery was backed up by true performance with 0–60mph coming in about 7sec. Dodge built 468 Hemi Chargers for 1966 and a mere twenty-seven the following year.

The Charger's innovative interior featured two rear bucket seats that, along with the center armrest, folded to form a flat storage area accessible through the trunk. The view shown here is the passenger area of a 1967 Charger.

fact that lead to the development of the winged Daytona beginning in June 1969. With an aerodynamic snout and towering rear spoiler, the Charger Daytona was capable of 200mph on the high banks, as was Plymouth's 1970 Road Runner-based version, the Superbird. After shattering various NASCAR records, Mopar's winged warriors were banned following the 1970 season.

A totally restyled B-body emerged in 1971 as the Charger, Road Runner, and GTX made their last stand as truly muscular performers. Plymouth's GTX was discontinued after 1971, as were the tri-carb 440s and the vaunted Hemi. And once the relatively warm 340 small-block disappeared after 1973, Mopar's B-body performance tale officially came to a close.

Standard 1967 GTX features included "GTX" emblems on the fenders and deck lid, a racing-style pop-open gas cap, twin bright exhaust trumpets, and Red Streak rubber. Also standard was Chrysler's tough Torqueflite three-speed automatic, with a four-speed available at extra cost. Five-spoke Magnum 500 sport wheels and twin black stripes were also GTX options. "GTO owners had better look to their defenses," concluded *Car and Driver.*

Previous pages
Considered an "executive's hot rod," Plymouth's GTX made the scene in 1967 loaded with attractive equipment. A twin-scooped hood and an interior featuring somewhat plush appointments and a center console were certainly impressive, but the real news was the GTX's standard 375hp 440ci big-block V-8, subtly identified within the hood ornament. Heavy-duty suspension and beefy drum brakes were included as well, and if that wasn't enough, the optional 426 Hemi stood waiting in the wings. In all, Plymouth rolled out 11,970 440-equipped GTX hardtops and convertibles in 1967; another 108 hardtops and seventeen convertibles were built with the Hemi.

Used initially as a torque mill for Chrysler's luxury barges, the 440 was modified in 1967 and reintroduced as the Super Commando V-8, a 375hp big-block installed as standard equipment under the GTX's twin scoops. The Super

Commando package included revised valvetrain gear, free-flowing exhausts, and a windage tray in the oil pan. With 10.1:1 compression, the 375hp 440 produced 480lb-ft of torque at 3200rpm. According to *Car and Driver*, "The Plymouth boys have breathed new life into the old 440 engine to produce a new monster capable of blowing off everything including a street Hemi up to 100 mph."

Left
Plymouth's 1968 Road Runner—designed for
customers who preferred going fast but didn't like
paying for a lot of irrelevant extras—inspired a
rash of so-called "budget supercars" out of
Detroit. Dress-up items were kept to a bare
minimum, with design efforts instead concentrat-
ing on underhood contents. Standard power came
from a modified 383ci big-block featuring the
cam, heads, exhaust manifolds, and windage tray
from the big brother 440. A four-speed was also
standard. "The Road Runner is the simplest, most
brazenly pure, non-compromising supercar in
history," claimed *Motor Trend*. In a *Super Stock
& Drag Illustrated* test, a 335hp 383 Road Runner
put up a 14.27sec, 92mph ET.

Although Road Runners were relatively
affordable performance packages in standard
form, a long list of options promised to both raise
the bottom line as well as straight-line potential.
Most prominent on the list was the ever-present
425hp 426 Hemi, priced at roughly $715. Vari-
ous mandatory options accompanied the Hemi,
such as the $138.90 Sure-Grip Dana 60 rearend
with 3.54:1 gears, and drove the final tally for a
Hemi Road Runner well beyond the $2,986 base
price. Production of 1968 Road Runner Hemi
coupes was 840. Another 171 1968 hardtops—
a mid-year model featuring roll-down rear
windows instead of the original flip-out units—
were built with the 425hp "King Kong" V-8.

This impressive scoop, sealed to the Six Pack's large air cleaner by an equally large rubber doughnut, fed cool air directly to those three hungry Holleys. As *Car Life* explained, the scoop "gapes wide open, seemingly ready to ingest all that gets near it including water, dirt, or birds." Although there was no stopping the birds, any water that entered the works was drained away by special drain tubes in the bottom of the air cleaner.

Left
Beneath a 440 Six Pack's oval air cleaner hid these three Holley two-barrel carburetors, totalling 1350cfm, on an Edelbrock aluminum intake manifold. Compression and cam timing for the 390hp 440 Six Pack were the same as the 375hp 440 Magnum with its single Carter four-barrel, but various internal modifications gave the Six Pack version improved high-winding capability. Included were stiff Hemi valve springs, beefed-up rocker arms and connecting rods, and specially machined cam lobes and lifter surfaces to minimize wear due to high valve spring pressures. Maximum Six Pack horsepower came at 4700rpm, compared to 4000rpm for the Magnum 440.

Following page
Although Dodge's exceptionally attractive, restyled 1968 Charger looked sleek, it possessed all the aerodynamics of a brick on NASCAR's superspeedways. Weary of trailing Ford and Mercury on the NASCAR circuit, the Dodge boys placed a group of Charger R/Ts in the hands of Creative Industries in Detroit with the goal being to produce a run of wind-cheating NASCAR homologation models. The result was the Charger 500, an odd concoction marketed as a 1969 model. Up front, a Coronet grille with exposed headlights (all other Chargers had hideaway units) was mounted flush, while in back the tunneled rear window area was filled in and the window mounted flush. The Charger 500 was superior to standard models at high speeds, but aerodynamic responses from Ford made Dodge's first aero warrior obsolete almost before it hit the track

Along with the obvious body modifications, Charger 500s were identified by "500" lettering in the tail's bumblebee stripe and emblems in the grille and below the right taillight. Production of 1969 Charger 500s is estimated at 392 today, even though NASCAR rules specified a homologation minimum of 500 regular production models. Power came from either a 375hp 440 Magnum or the 425hp 426 Hemi. Reportedly, this Hemi-powered Charger 500 is one of sixty-seven known to exist.

Right
Two problems hindered the redesigned 1968 Charger's performance on NASCAR superspeedways: the recessed grille up front served as an anchor as it trapped airflow, while the stylish tunneled rear window area created turbulence, which translated into serious drag. To solve the problem in back, Creative Industries' people fabricated a steel plug to fill in the tunneled backlight, then added a flush-mounted rear window. A similar tactic was applied to the 1969 Daytona and 1970 Superbird.

Ford Motor Company's response to the Charger 500 was the 1969 Talladega and Cyclone Spoiler II, sleek, slippery stockers that forced Dodge designers back to the drawing board. The result was the radical Charger Daytona. Keeping the Charger 500's steel rear window plug, the Daytona also featured a highly aerodynamic steel nose cone and a wild aluminum rear wing. Although the street versions didn't require them, the rear-facing fender scoops needed to clear the oversized tires on racing Daytonas were retained. Dodge built 503 Charger Daytonas in 1969.

Dodge's second aerodynamic NASCAR variant was available to streetside customers with either a 375hp 440 Magnum or 425hp 426 Hemi under the hood. Production was 433 for the 440-equipped Daytonas, and seventy for the Hemi cars. Rarity in the case of this particular Daytona is intensified by its paint scheme. This Bright Seafoam Turquoise Metallic finish, coded Q5, is only known on one other 1969 Daytona.

Right
Like the Charger 500, the Charger Daytona was built by Creative Industries in Detroit. Thanks to its high-flying "towel rack" spoiler and distinctive snout, the Daytona reportedly possessed an excellent 0.29 coefficient of drag. Throw in 426 Hemi power at the track and 200mph was no problem.

Left
Plymouth produced a winged wonder of its own in 1970, applying similar tactics used by the '69 Charger Daytona to its revamped Road Runner body. But while Dodge only had to build 500 Daytonas to make them legal for NASCAR competition, sanctioning officials raised the ante to 1000 in 1970. No problem, Plymouth ended up selling 1,935 Superbirds; 1,084 with the 375hp 440, 716 with the 390hp 440 Six Barrel, and 135 with the 425hp 426 Hemi. After dominating the 1970 NASCAR season, Mopar's winged warriors were banned from competition, transforming the1970 Superbird into a one-year wonder.

Although both Dodge's Daytona and Plymouth's Superbird appeared similar, minor differences in design dominated. Up front, the steel nose cones varied slightly in shape and the Superbird's air inlet—shown here—was located below the tip (Daytona inlets wrapped up slightly to the top side). Both cars used the same fiberglass hideaway headlight buckets, but the Superbird's fender scoops were rounded while the Daytona's were flat on top. In back, the Superbird's wing was taller and swept back further than the Daytona's. Unlike Daytonas, Superbirds also needed vinyl tops to hide required lead work in the rear window area.

The last of Plymouth's GTX models, the 1971 edition, impressed many as a muscle car survivor at a time when factory performance was clearly on the wane. As *Car and Driver's* staff wrote, "we would have to say that the GTX is a step forward on a front where all others are retreating. It is vastly improved over the previous model and only in performance, primarily because of increased weight, has it lost ground." Serious performance buyers could still order the 390hp 440+6 and 425hp Hemi, but a mere 135 chose the tri-carb 440 and only thirty selected the Hemi.

Left
A totally new, bulging body may have helped appearances, but Plymouth's 1971 GTX suffered slightly from the addition of 170 extra pounds and minor detuning of the standard 440 big-block. *Road & Track's* best quarter-mile effort in a 1971 GTX was 14.40sec at 98.7mph showing the 440-powered B-body was still no slouch. This 1971 GTX is one of 2,538 built with the standard 440.

Left
By 1971, increasingly restrictive emissions standards were taking their toll on factory performance as compression ratios started dropping and smog equipment began strangling the last breath out of American muscle cars. Nonetheless, Chrysler stood relatively firm for at least one more year, and Plymouth's veteran 440 Super Commando only lost 5hp in 1971, down to 370 thanks to a compression decrease to 9.7:1.

A retyled, curvaceous body also graced Dodge's 1971 Charger, a Coke-bottle-shaped creation that rolled on a wheelbase two inches shorter than previous editions. Carried over on the new platform was the Charger R/T featuring heavy-duty suspension, various exterior identification including distinctive "door gills" and a blacked-out hood section, and the 370hp 440 Magnum V-8. Also continued into 1971 were the optional 440 Six Pack and 426 Hemi powerplants. Total production of R/T Chargers in 1971 was 3,118.

Loaded with an incredible array of options, including an exceedingly rare power sunroof (only three 1971 Hemi Chargers had this fitted), this Hemi-powered Charger R/T carried a hefty $6,380.60 sticker in 1971. Base price for the Charger R/T was $3,777. Notice the dictation machine at the head of the console. The orange knob below the steering column activates the toothy hood flap.

Right
Surviving for one last year, the famed Hemi received hydraulic valve lifters in 1971, but remained at its intimidating 425hp. Performance for a 1971 Hemi Charger was equally intimidating, registering in the high 13sec range for the quarter-mile. Only sixty-three Hemi Chargers were built for 1971; thirty-three with Torqueflites, thirty with four-speeds.

Index